# EMPIRE GHOSTS

## NEW YORK STATE'S HAUNTED LANDMARKS

## LYNDA LEE MACKEN

# EMPIRE GHOSTS

ISBN 0-9700718-8-4

Cover design:
Debra Tremper, Six Penny Graphics
Fredericksburg, VA

Back cover logo design:
Glenda Moore, catStuff Graphics

Printed on recycled paper by
Sheridan Books, Fredericksburg, VA

## CONTENTS

## INTRODUCTION

Spiritualism debuted in New York State in 1848, when Catherine and Margaretta Fox claimed they had contacted a deceased peddler through a series of knocks. They took their show on the road and became an international sensation sparking the country's interest in spiritualism.

For the next fifty years people eagerly engaged in séances and table rapping in an effort to communicate with the dead.

Long before the Fox Sisters rapped with "Mr. Splitfoot," ghosts inhabited New York's landscape. The Empire State is populated with hundreds of phantoms but the spirits presented in *Empire Ghosts* are exceptional for their notoriety and longevity.

At its heart, *Empire Ghosts* merges history with the mysteries of New York State where the supernatural is an enchanting and hidden treasure.

I grew up on Staten Island fascinated by ghosts but reluctant to ever see one. Fate dealt a different hand and in 1988, while vacationing at Covewood Lodge on Big Moose Lake in the Adirondack Mountains, Grace Brown's ghost manifested before my eyes. Ultimately the story was told on *Unsolved Mysteries* and in *Adirondack Ghosts*, sparking a new career chronicling ghost stories.

Ghosts are caught in a netherland; they are confused beings who don't realize they're dead. Such is the case with poor Malinda Van Horn who died at the tender age of 21 when she was struck in the head by a tree limb, and George Fykes, a soldier killed in His Majesty's Service at

While I nodded, nearly napping, suddenly there came a tapping, as of some one gently rapping, rapping at my bedroom door.

~ Edgar Allan Poe

*"Birthplace of Spiritualism"*
*Newark, New York*

Fort Ontario, and Tanya the lonely five-year-old haunting Grand Island's Holiday Inn.

Some spirits stay behind out of a sense of duty like the one that shows up as an inexplicable orb of light hovering over the sentries walking the ramparts at the Youngstown fort; the Country House Restaurant's revolutionary Annette Williamson; an unknown soldier at West Point; or the State Capitol's night watchman.

It would appear that there are those who remain behind purely to show their displeasure with changes in their mortal environments such as Mrs. Stacey at the Bull's Head Inn or the White Inn's unhappy Isabel.

Some events are imprinted on the environment and materialize over and over intensifying as witnesses react to them,[1] like Abraham Lincoln's funeral train, "Mad" Anthony Wayne's midnight ride, or Split Rock quarry's fiery disaster.

At this point in time, true hauntings exist in the realm of the unknown and perhaps we may never solve their mystery. One thing is certain however, they remain a fascinating subject and, for believers, they provide a certain comfort that life *does* go on after death.

---

[1] Sylvia Brown, *Visits from the Afterlife.*

*T*here must be ghosts all over the world.
They must be as countless as the grains of the sand,
it seems to me.

~ Henrik Ibsen, *Ghosts*

*New York State Capitol*

## NEW YORK STATE CAPITOL BUILDING
### *Albany*

Located at the State Street end of the Empire State Plaza, this magnificent red-towered building boasts hundreds of arched windows and unlike most capitol buildings, the 1868 structure is French Renaissance style and doesn't possess the traditional dome.

Construction on the edifice began in 1899 and was completed 30 years later for the then outrageous sum of $25 million.

Built in the tradition of great medieval cathedrals, many stone carvings grace the interior and are caricatures of famous politicians, writers, and some self-portraits of the carvers themselves. The centerpiece of the structure is the magnificent "Million-Dollar Staircase," which took years to complete.

Governors Theodore Roosevelt, Franklin D. Roosevelt and Nelson Rockefeller occupied offices in the building to execute their official duties.

A ghostly janitor, known as "George," is long on overtime. Moans, clanking keys, rattling doorknobs, muffled voices, and furtive shadows are some of the strange phenomena that for years have plagued the Assembly Chamber.

Some after-hours staff members have requested reassignment after encountering George's spine-chilling apparition roaming the fifth floor.

A professional psychic feels the earthbound spirit is Samuel J. Abbott, a night watchman who perished in the 1911 Capitol fire.

Pour forth your poison, our deliverance!
This fire consumes our minds, let's bid adieu,
Plumb Hell or Heaven, what's the difference?
Plumb the Unknown, to find out something new!

~ Charles Baudelaire

*The New York State Capitol Assembly Chamber*

## NEW YORK CENTRAL RAILROAD TRACKS

One of the Empire State's well-established ghost stories is that on April 27th of every year, the fleeting image of Abraham Lincoln's funeral train runs on New York Central Railroad's Hudson River Division railroad tracks.

After Lincoln was assassinated on April 14, 1865, a train covered in black crepe transported his body 1,700 miles from Washington, D.C. through the New York State countryside en route to his burial place in Springfield, Illinois.

Legend says the ghost train, seen in the Capital District, carries an ethereal ensemble that plays eerie funeral dirges as a crew of skeletons conducts the train.

*New York Central Railroad Station, Albany*

7

*Cherry Hill*

## CHERRY HILL
### *Albany*

In 1787, Philip Van Rensselaer's 31-room Georgian mansion, at 523½ South Pearl Street, was the centerpiece of his 900-acre farm. For five generations the Van Rensselaer family inhabited the grand Cherry Hill estate. By 1963, the family sold the surrounding land and an urban neighborhood developed around the house.

Although the orchards no longer exist and the view from the stoop is of railroad yards, not farmyards, the house retains its dignity and elegance - and a presence from the past.

For many years, neighborhood residents reported a ghostly figure wandering the lower floor and walking on the terrace. The specter's identity remains a mystery however.

The fact is that on May 7, 1827 migrant worker Jesse Strang murdered the Van Rensselaer's manager, John Whipple.

The prevailing tale is that Strang was a ne'er do well who had a fling with Whipple's wife. She persuaded Jesse to kill her husband so that they could be together. Strang purchased a pistol and shot Whipple through a window as the diligent and trustworthy manager sat with his employer going over accounts. Whipple died instantly.

Strang was immediately apprehended, tried and convicted. He was sentenced to the gallows and penned his confession before he was hanged (a copy exists at

Cherry Hill). Strang was the last person to be publicly executed in New York State.

Mrs. Whipple was sentenced to jail time for the part she played in the crime.

The question remains - *who* is haunting Cherry Hill? Some say it's the convicted murderer. Perhaps his spirit is imprinted on the environment, caught in an endless loop, and continues to pace outside on the terrace waiting for a rendezvous with his lover, or for a clear shot at his victim.

More likely though, the restless wraith is John Whipple. Cut down by surprise in the prime of his life, it's likely his conscientious spirit stays behind to keep an eye on Van Rensselaer's estate, as was his charge in life.

## *USS THE SULLIVANS*
### *Buffalo*

The five Sullivan brothers thought they were invincible as long as they stuck together.

Albert, Francis, George, Joseph and Madison Sullivan were born in Waterloo, Iowa, between 1914 and 1920. During World War II they enlisted in the U. S. Navy on one condition - that they serve on the same ship. Even though this was against naval policy, all five brothers were stationed on the *USS Juneau.*

Four of the Sullivan brothers died when their cruiser was torpedoed on Friday, November 13, 1942. For the next few days, the eldest and only surviving brother, George, went from life raft to life raft desperately searching for his deceased brothers. A shark attacked the delirious man as he attempted to swim to a remote island.

The country was outraged over what had happened. Never again would the Navy allow family members to be stationed together in a war zone.

The Navy decided to honor the five Sullivan brothers by naming a new destroyer *USS The Sullivans* on February 10, 1943. The vessel is unique for several reasons. This was the first time the Navy used the word "the" in the name of a ship, shamrocks adorn the smokestack, and five men who never set foot on it haunt it.

Thirty-five years after it was commissioned, the destroyer was donated to New York State and established as a memorial in the Buffalo and Erie County Naval and Servicemen's Park.

Workers aboard the mothballed ship say that the spirits of the five brothers make themselves known in some way every Friday the 13th. Five luminous forms have been discerned floating down passageways; chilling, disembodied whispers of "Hey, You!" and sounds of men playing cards have been heard.

The terrible specter of George, the oldest Sullivan brother, his face and clothes bloodied and badly burned, was sighted floating above the deck and caused a worker to quit his job on the spot. When photos are taken of the portrait of the five brothers, George's image oftentimes comes out as a white blur.

Caretakers find locked doors unlocked, items fly across the room, and radar is activated when there is no electrical power to run it.

## ATHENAEUM HOTEL
### *Chautauqua*

From Ulysses S. Grant to Bill Clinton, nine presidents have visited the famous Athenaeum Hotel. Other notables include Marion Anderson, Susan B. Anthony, and Robert Kennedy. What is uncertain is the number of spirits who stay over at the Victorian inn.

In the southwestern corner of New York State, "La Grande Dame of Chautauqua" sits atop a tree-shaded hill overlooking picturesque Chautauqua Lake on the grounds of the internationally recognized Chautauqua Institution.

Since 1881, guests have vacationed at the historic landmark and a story exists about one who never left.

The traditional tale, according to *Spirits of the Great Hill* (Winfield), is about a curious little girl on her tricycle exploring the many recesses about the great guesthouse. When she spied a pair of open elevator doors, she rode right in and, tragically, down the shaft to her death.

There are those who swear the haunting tinkle of the tyke's tricycle bell faintly chimes throughout the halls.

## BULL'S HEAD INN
### *Cobleskill*

The oldest building in the village of Cobleskill is also its most haunted. The Bull's Head Inn opened its doors to the public in 1802 but forty years later it was converted into a private residence.

In 1966 when it again opened as a restaurant, silverware, plates, and napkins started flying about. When the apparition of a woman in white showed up in the previous resident's bedroom, it became apparent the ghostly culprit was Mrs. John Stacey.

Mrs. Stacy lived in the Federal Georgian style house at 2 Park Place from 1920 to 1966. A woman of self-restraint she was a loyal member of the Women's Christian Temperance Union. Most agree her displeasure with drinking stems from her days with Mr. Stacey who tippled a little too much.

Seeing strangers guzzle in her former home gets Stacey's ghost going. Captain's chairs swivel without explanation and an old crank phone, that hasn't worked in years, will sometimes ring.

While dining, a couple sat dumbfounded as a plate lifted off their table and flew across the room. Workers claim to see a shadowy shape out of the corners of their eyes or a vague figure in mirrors. After closing, one worker saw Stacey's ethereal form floating behind the bar.

Most times the creepiness intensifies when late night revelers are reluctant to leave the old-time watering hole.

## HYDE HALL
*Cooperstown*

When her thankless children evicted Ann Cooper Clarke from her house in 1800, she threatened to return and haunt it forever. The aristocratic Clarke family's long residence at Hyde Hall provides a remarkable record of over 250 years of New York State history and almost certainly guarantees a legacy of spirits left behind to inhabit the ancestral home.

George Clarke inherited his proper English family's vast real estate holdings (120,000 acres) and sugar cane fortune from Jamaican plantations, and commissioned the construction of a magnificent estate on a hillside overlooking Otsego Lake.

Philip Hooker, a leading New York architect, designed the impressive showplace that today is considered the finest example of neoclassic country mansions anywhere in America. Hyde is composed of four structures, containing 50 rooms that enclose an open courtyard. This design set the structure apart from other American dwellings.

Clarke divorced his wife in 1813 (she refused to come to America) and married Ann Corey Cooper, the widow of James Fenimore Cooper's brother. When he died in 1835, he left his mansion and a portion of his fortune to his son George Clarke, Jr.

George Jr. was a debonair young man who dabbled in risky enterprises. When the hops market collapsed in the late 19th century, George Jr. lost his investment and then some. He filed bankruptcy and relinquished the mansion.

George Jr.'s son, George Hyde Clarke married into the Averell Carter family and his mother-in-law bought back the grand home and all of its contents.

Hyde Hall was home to Clarke and his descendants for three generations and stands as a reminder of an era when British nobility created great estates in the former colonies.[2] The Clarke family is one of the few who managed to hold on to their assets during the tumult of the American Revolution.

New York State acquired the 3,000-acre property in 1963 for the development of Glimmerglass State Park. Time and lack of maintenance had taken their toll on the building and the state had no resources for restoration. The grand home was facing demolition.

Fortunately "Friends of Hyde Hall" took charge and saved the house. In 1988, the non-profit organization gained full responsibility for the structure's restoration and management.

Visitors who tour the structure today can observe the faithful restoration in progress and they may also sense a presence from the past.

In *Ghosts of the Northeast,* author David Pitkin says the last remaining Clarkes asserted that their Alsatian dog refused to go down a rear stairway and snarled as if warding off an unwanted intruder. Often the sound of disembodied footsteps was heard on this staircase as well as the main staircase outside the billiard room.

Pitkin explored the house, along with an intuitive friend, and gained a unique paranormal perspective. The sensitive discerned the imprints of a festive Christmas celebration, lively political discussions in the library, and the image of a young woman concerned about the welfare

---

[2] www.hydehall.org

of a soldier fighting the Civil War (two Clarke family members died in the war between the states).

Workers renovating the house spied a dusty cloud take on an ethereal form and "swoosh" up a hallway. Speculation has it that the wraith may be the spirit of Arthur Sherwood, a family friend who died of heart failure in the house.

In 1921, James Fenimore Cooper's grandson and namesake initially recorded the hauntings of Hyde Hall in *The Legends and Traditions of a Northern County.*

Cooper, staying overnight in the blue room, claimed to see the specter of an older man. When he shared his experience with his hostess the next morning, she concurred that indeed the appearance of a ghost in this little used room, once the sleeping quarters of George Clarke, was common.

The frequently sighted specter dressed in a yellow, red, and green "wrapper," would walk down the hall and enter his former bedroom. Since Clarke's colorful robe was packed away in a household trunk, the family felt certain the spook was their ancestor.

(Photo source: www.hydehall.org)

When the footpads quail at the night bird's wail,
And black dogs bay at the moon,
Then is the specters' holiday – then is the ghosts'
high noon!

~ Sir William Schwenck Gilbert
*Ruddigore*

(U.S. Coast Guard Photo)

*Fire Island Lighthouse*

## FIRE ISLAND LIGHTHOUSE
### *Fire Island*

Long before Fire Island became a popular summer destination, the mysterious island was a desolate place where pirates, wreckers, and the ghosts of their victims wandered.

The first Fire Island Lighthouse was built in 1825; the foundation just a few steps from the present black-banded lighthouse completed in 1858.

Local lore says that the caretaker of the 1825 light hanged himself and the old keeper's spirit moved in to haunt the present station.

Supernatural accounts of heavy doors slamming are baffling; no wind is strong enough to blow the heavy portals open. Who, or what, can explain this mystery? Another oddity is that at times the topmost windows rise by themselves when normally a special tool is required to reach them.

People have reported the sounds of unusual laughter and someone knocking when no one else is in the beacon. Unaccountable cold spots persist throughout the light, a common signal that a ghost is present.

Although not directly attributable to the haunting activity here, another eerie occurrence is that human skulls and various other skeleton parts have washed up on the beach directly in front of the lighthouse.

The bones are thought to be the mortal remains of prisoners and slaves once confined to ships moored off the Long Island coast.

*I*t is an unwise man
who thinks that what has changed is dead.

~ Anonymous

*The White Inn*

## THE WHITE INN
### *Fredonia*

*Mayflower* descendant, Dr. Squire White, was the first medical doctor to settle and practice in Chautauqua County. In 1811 he erected a wood frame house on the site of today's White Inn.

When fire destroyed the home, Dr. White's son, Devillo, built a more substantial structure, the foundation of what was to become the landmark inn.

In 1918, the last remaining White family resident sold the property to Murray Hill Bartley who expanded the property and opened a hotel for the traveling public.

Located along scenic Route 20, a one-time main thoroughfare, the White Inn flourished and became a favored gathering spot. Duncan Hines discovered the White Inn in the 1930's, and was so impressed with the restaurant that he included the inn as one of 50 exceptional establishments that grew to be his "Family of Fine Restaurants."

Physics discern entities in the place but only one sighting of a full-bodied apparition was ever reported - that of a filmy young girl with arms outstretched.

The oddest manifestation took place in a room of the Presidential Suite. The huge commotion sounded as if furniture was being rearranged. When the door was opened all was still except for a rotating light.

Most of the harmless haunting activity is limited to this room where the culprit, suspected to be Isabel, the relative who sold the property to Bartley, continues to show her displeasure with its conversion to a guesthouse.

## BELHURST CASTLE
### Geneva

*M*ystery and intrigue swirl about the ivy-covered stone mansion perched on a cliff above Seneca Lake. Long before the turreted castle was constructed Seneca Indians inhabited the property and the site was home to the Council of the Six Nations of Iroquois.

In the early 1700s, the land was part of the state of Massachusetts and a hundred years later the Ontario Glass Manufacturing Company, the first glass company west of Albany, flourished there.

At the turn of the 19th century, William Henry Bucke resided in the "Hermitage," a home built by the previous owner of the property. He used the alias of Henry Hall, but most people knew him as Bucke Hall. Many believed Hall built a tunnel as a means of escape via the lake if authorities ever found him.

Upon his death, it was discovered that Hall had been treasurer of the famed Covent Garden Theater in London. The story goes that he embezzled theater funds, married his stepmother, fled to the United States and assumed the name Henry Hall in order to avoid arrest.

For 30 years after Hall's death in 1836, the property changed hands several times and eventually became known as "Otis Grove," a popular picnic area for Geneva residents. The "Hermitage" was still intact and it was rumored then that the house was haunted.

By 1885, new owner Carrie Harron, who divorced her husband and married her manager, started to erect the four-story mansion.

Fifty men worked four years to construct Belhurst Castle. During this time, one man was killed when he fell from the tower and a roofer went insane. Most of the materials used to build and furnish the castle were imported to Geneva from Europe.

In the 1930s, Belhurst operated as a speakeasy and gambling casino. During prohibition, liquor was run down from Canada using the canal system. By 1952, the Kefauver Commission effectively ended the gambling.

Belhurst continued as a restaurant and in 1975 the property was renovated to accommodate overnight guests. The 112-year-old Romanesque-style inn boasts a four-diamond rating and a history of hauntings.

The story of the spectral white lady is legendary and a phantom nanny and gambler keep her wraith company.

The white lady is said to be the spirit of an Italian opera singer who fled from Spain with her lover to escape scandal. Eventually they were found out by their pursuers and supposedly the couple died while hiding out in the secret tunnel when it collapsed.

Although this tale has no basis in history, over the years, dozens of guests have reported seeing a woman in white standing on the front lawn over the area where the tunnel was dug.

Sometimes when there are no children present at the inn, a woman's voice is faintly heard singing a soothing lullaby.

Dick O'Brien, a friend of the castle's owner during its prohibition days, allegedly died of a heart attack in the men's room. Sightings of his pale apparition add to the mystical history of Belhurst Castle.

*Winfield Hall*

## WINFIELD HALL
### Glen Cove

In the early 20th century, more than any other region, Long Island's "Gold Coast" glittered with private mansions, country clubs, polo fields, and marinas. Fabulously wealthy estate owners tried to outdo each other in displays of opulence.

Winfield Hall was F. W. Woolworth's magnificent attempt at luxury. Among the many extravagances in his 62-room mansion at 77 Crescent Beach Road were solid gold bathroom fixtures and a dining room ceiling gilded with 1,500 square feet of fourteen-carat gold.

The misty apparitions of the 5 & 10 cent store magnate and his daughter, Edna Winfield, who committed suicide in the house, appeared during séances held in the 1917 mansion.

Woolworth died only two years after he built the elaborate home. A known eccentric, he was too afraid to go to the dentist and succumbed to infection caused by his decaying teeth.

The Italian Renaissance manse provided the perfect backdrop for the supernatural strains of spectral organ music said to fill the spacious structure on occasion.

Edna committed suicide in the house and an oft-told tale is that the family's coat of arms cracked through the likeness of Edna's face that was etched on the seal the night she killed herself.

Today the imposing edifice stands empty - *or does it?*

## MORGAN HALL
### *Glen Cove*

Between 1900 and the end of World War I, Long Island saw unprecedented development. The North Shore of this rural community of farmers and fishermen was transformed into an exclusive country retreat and was dubbed the "Gold Coast."

During this time, sixty of America's richest men erected estates here - among them, banker John Pierpont Morgan.

After his death, the spirit of the famous financier took up permanent residence in his 1910 Nassau County estate.

The Russian Embassy held title to the property for a while and then the Catholic Church took over ownership. The nuns complained about loud disembodied footsteps echoing throughout the cavernous halls and in the attic at odd hours during the night.

In October 1965, windows on the third floor slowly slid open on their own then slammed shut.

The most unnerving ghostly manifestation was the figure of an aged old man, thought to be J. P. himself, floating through the rooms leaving an icy chill in his wake.

The poltergeist activity was originally attributed to Morgan, but a young female apparition wearing a long black gown started to appear to the novitiates. Psychics identified the specter as Alice, Morgan's daughter, who died of typhoid fever.

## HOLIDAY INN
### Grand Island

The ghost at the Grand Island Holiday Inn on Whitehaven Road is a little girl the staff has named "Tanya." The hotel has so many reports about the ghost from guests and staff that they could "fill a book."

The story goes that Tanya died in a fire that occurred in the house that once stood on the property. She is about five yeas old, with long wild tresses and wears a red dress and black button shoes. She's shy and sensitive - if you yell at her because of her antics she'll quiet down for a few days, but soon will be up to her old tricks again.

Mostly Tanya can be found running up and down the halls, bouncing a ball, or jumping on beds. Her favorite room is #422 where guests once complained to the front desk that they found a young girl in their room playing with their children's toys.

Housekeepers attest to seeing the lonely girl's ghost wandering the hallways crying "I'm lost" or hearing the little child's voice call them by name.

## BANNERMAN'S ISLAND
*Hudson River*

Native Americans long suspected that the tiny island in the Hudson River was haunted and dared to visit only during daylight.

Early Dutch settlers thought the island was possessed by goblins who controlled the difficult river passage where unpredictable winds could capsize their boats.

In 1900, Francis Bannerman purchased the 6.5-acre island to store his large supply of weapons and war-related items; his business was dealing in war surplus.

Bannerman constructed warehouses and eventually a Scottish-style castle for his family. (One warehouse was whitewashed and painted with the Manhattan address of his retail store - the first Army & Navy store).

In order to build docks, Bannerman bought old ships, sunk them and covered them up with concrete.[3]

A tugboat captain, particularly fond of his craft, asked workers to wait until he was far downriver before they sunk his beloved boat. Unbelievably, the ship went down before he could turn away. Furious with their lack of empathy, he cursed the crew and Bannerman too, shouting they had not heard the last of him.

A lodge was built over the drowned tug and for years workers heard the distinctive double ring of a ship's bell - the signal that a boat was going in reverse. All believed the ethereal ringing was the spirit of the angry captain eternally reversing his boat to get it away from the island.

---

[3] Linda Zimmerman, *Hauntings of the Hudson Valley.*

## LINDENWALD ESTATE
### *Kinderhook*

Lindenwald estate presents a retrospective on President Martin Van Buren's thirty years of public service and provides an incredible insight into the past.

Originally built as a Dutch farmhouse by Judge William Peter Van Ness in 1797, some of the spectral activity inside the home is attributed to his insolent son, John. An incorrigible gambler, he lost the property in a card game to Leonard Jerome. Although, not related to its haunted history, it bears mentioning that Jerome's daughter gave birth to Winston Churchill.

The sounds of disembodied footsteps and slamming doors throughout the house, reported by former residents, are attributed to son John's annoyance over losing the comfy roof over his head.

Aaron Burr is New York's most extraordinary ghost - his tormented specter shows up in many places all over the state including Kinderhook.

Burr evaded authorities by hiding out in the Van Ness estate after his fatal duel with Alexander Hamilton. Despite the fact that the secret room was added to the house after Burr's get-away, a long-held tradition affirms that when the hidden attic room was discovered, a rocking chair, a whittled wooden pig, and a faded calling card with the name "Aaron Burr" was found leading to the belief that Burr was holed up in the tiny space during his three year hiatus.

Nevertheless, Burr's apparition *did* appear in the apple orchard dressed in a dark red coat and ruffled shirt.

*T*he sleeping and the dead are but as pictures.

~ William Shakespeare

*Lindenwald Estate*

The eighth president of the United States, Martin Van Buren, descended from an Old Dutch family and was born in Kinderhook in 1782. Van Buren served as a United States Senator, New York governor, Secretary of State, Vice-president, and became the first New Yorker to become President of the United States (1837-1841).

The former president retired to his hometown and ended up purchasing and renovating the Van Ness estate. Lindenwald is named after the trees on the property and Van Buren's specter was also seen afoot in the orchard.

Lindenwald's orchard may be a magnet for the paranormal because a third ghost inhabited the grove. Not long after a morose butler hung himself from one of the fruit trees, his specter was sighted swinging from a limb.

The most delectable supernatural demonstration, and the one most often experienced at Lindenwald on Sunday mornings, is the aroma of pancakes sizzling on a buttered skillet. Could it be Aunt Sarah cooking up a stack from beyond the grave?

Aunt Sarah was a free slave who worked at the estate for many years. Her culinary skill was renowned and she ruled her kitchen with an iron hand. Many feel her spirit remains attached to her earthly domain.

A hydrothermalgraph monitors the temperature and humidity inside the historic house museum and produces charts delineating the measurements for 24 hours. In *Hauntings of the Hudson Valley*, Linda Zimmerman writes that on one New Year's Eve, the temperature spiked inside the dwelling as if warm-blooded individuals were present for several hours, even though the staff found no evidence, or possible entry, of any interlopers.

Now *there's* a party I'm sorry I missed!

*Selkirk Lighthouse*

## SELKIRK LIGHTHOUSE
### *Lake Ontario*

First visited by Samuel de Champlain in 1615, the site of the Selkirk Light hosted an important assembly of Cayuga, Oneida and Onondaga tribes that resulted in a treaty with the French during the French and Indian War.

New York Governor George Clinton purchased the property north of the Salmon River from the three tribes in 1788 and soon the first permanent white settlement was established, the excellent Atlantic salmon fishing being the draw.

During the War of 1812, the waterfront became a haven for smugglers and then bootleggers throughout prohibition over a century later.

In the early 1830's the construction of a lighthouse, complete with a customs office, was underway to shore up the flourishing shipping and fishing industries.

The automated Selkirk Light is one of only four remaining "birdcage lantern" style lights and is the only existing lighthouse with a wood floored watchtower and staircase.

Along with its maritime history, the lighthouse harbors a *haunted* history as well. For years mariners have marveled over the "ghost lady" of Selkirk Lighthouse.

When observed she is always wearing a vintage, full-length dress. Some say she's a captain's daughter still on the lookout for her father's ship to return.

Another account claims she is a former keeper's daughter who, as she was taking her father supper, tripped and fell to her death down the spiral staircase.

What are these,
So withered, and so wild in their attire,
That look not like th' inhabitants o' th' earth,
And yet are on't?

~ William Shakespeare
*Macbeth*

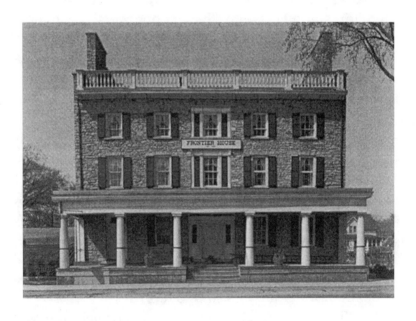

*Frontier House*

## FRONTIER HOUSE
### *Lewiston*

Yes, even McDonalds restaurant serves up ghosts...

Lewiston's 1824 Frontier House was at one time a highbrow hotel and the westernmost stop of the Barton Stage Line. Notables such as DeWitt Clinton, Edward Prince of Wales, James Fennimore Cooper, President McKinley, Jenny Lind, and Henry Clay, among others, visited the old lodging.

When the place operated as a hotel, former managers claimed that doors opened and closed on their own. The inn once served as a Masonic meeting lodge and some suspect the ancient building may be the postmortem home of William Morgan.

Morgan was a controversial figure who mysteriously disappeared in 1826 after threatening to publish an exposé of the Masons. Some attribute the odd goings-on to the long gone agitator.

When spirits are embedded in a structure renovations often release them as evidenced during the numerous refurbishments of the Frontier House. Frustrated laborers, transforming the place into a McDonald's restaurant, felt certain the structure was haunted when their tools disappeared and the electrical power failed without explanation.

A female janitor regularly witnessed a male apparition in vintage clothing and a customer reported the specter of a man standing in the bathroom. One shaken maintenance worker walked out and never came back because he was so unnerved by the building.

## BEARDSLEE CASTLE
### Little Falls

$A$ugustus Beardslee built the spooky looking castle on Route 5 between Little Falls and St. Johnsville in the 1860s to replicate an Irish fortress. His son, Captain Guy Roosevelt Beardslee was born in the mansion and graduated West Point; he supervised the completion of the edifice, which ultimately became the region's social center[4].

Every stone used for the structure was quarried right on the property and was hand cut by Swiss stonemasons. More than a mile of stone walls surround the park-like setting and add to its eerie appearance.

Beardslee constructed a dam and power plant to furnish power and light, not only for his own farms, but also for the Village of St. Johnsville. "Street" lights turned on in St. Johnsville on March 17, 1898.

According to historical records there was a small fort on the site about 1750, when the Mohawk Valley was wilderness. Legend has it that a tunnel led from the house into a hill where a supply of munitions was stored. During a raid on the fortress, Indians accidentally set off the gunpowder with their torches and were blown to bits.

The burrow's entrance is in Beardslee's basement and sealed off by boulders. Some think the ghosts here could be restless Indian spirits. Since the house was part of the Underground Railroad, slaves could have hidden out in the tunnel and their spirits may linger here as well.

---

[4]Arthur Myers, *Ghostly American Places*.

A Beardslee son drowned nearby and the boy's spirit is often heard playing in the building, but is never found.

Legend says that Captain Beardslee's ghoul roams the grounds at night carrying a lantern to light his way. Several auto accidents in the area have been attributed to Beardslee's ghost and his confounding light.

All manner of unexplained phenomena occurs at the creepy castle and is ascribed to a hefty number of ghosts.

"Pop" Anton M. Christensen purchased the property from Mrs. Beardslee and opened the mansion as a restaurant in 1941. He suffered from depression and ended up committing suicide by hanging. His frightening specter shows up dangling from a noose in the dark recess upstairs where he took his life.

Employees hear indiscernible voices and footsteps resounding after the restaurant closes, orbs of light float through the rooms, lights are found on when turned off the night before, doors locked at night are unlocked in the morning, and an ungodly shriek, called the "Big Scream," resonates throughout the structure, its source unknown.

One employee shared that she suddenly felt icy cold and looked down to see a disembodied hand that looked like an x-ray image - she could see the bones.[5] Soon after, a co-worker saw a man dressed in a top hat and black suit standing in the same archway where the hand appeared; the "Abe Lincoln-like" image quickly dissolved.

A party guest captured the same dark apparition on film. Sightings of this entity have a long history and those in the know identify him as Dominie Jake, a disgraceful deacon who was accused of molesting children, according

---

[5]Ibid.

to the castle's chronicles.[6]    The shamed clergyman purportedly hung himself in the underground passageway.

An odd cast of ghostly characters calls the castle home. There's the specter who sits in a wingback chair by the fireplace even though, in reality, there is no seating arranged there. A flaxen-haired wraith in a full-length dress frequents the ladies room. One worker saw a woman in a dressing gown carrying a bed tray up an invisible flight of stairs (before the remodel, a staircase existed there).

Once when a diner used an upstairs restroom he peered into the banquet room and saw a foursome enjoying a candlelight dinner. He mentioned it to his server and together they went to investigate - the room was empty.

"Abigail" is yet another presence who supposedly was a servant at the manor who choked and died. Her spirit calls out to the help whispering their names and giving them the heebie-jeebies.

Although most of the mysterious activity takes place during off hours, not surprisingly, Beardslee Castle attracts a large number of ghost hunters. These serious investigators have attempted to record electronic voice phenomena (EVP). Their chilling recordings captured ghostly voices from the past whispering, "Why," and "Who is that person?"

The History Channel produced a segment about Beardslee's ghosts as part of its popular *Haunted History* series. The spooky episode premiered in October 1999 and can still be seen in re-run.

---

[6] Ibid.

## LOUDON COTTAGE
### *Loudonville*

*B*orn in 1845, Clara Harris was the daughter of New York senator Ira Harris. When her mother passed away, her father remarried the mother of Major Henry Rathbone.

Abraham Lincoln's wife, Mary, invited Clara and Henry Rathbone, to Washington's Ford Theatre, on April 14, 1865, to see the play *Our American Cousin*.

During the third act, John Wilkes Booth entered Lincoln's box and shot the president in the back of the head. Henry Rathbone attempted to subdue the assassin, but Booth slashed Rathbone's arm with a hunting knife. A struggle ensued that resulted in Booth's inability to cleanly jump from the State Box. Booth landed on the stage eleven feet below at an awkward angle and fractured his ankle. He was, however, able to hobble out and escape on horseback.

Clara, who was sitting nearby, would never forget that awful night. She was so close to President Lincoln that his blood splattered on her dress.

When Clara returned to her parents' home in Loudonville, she hung her stained dress in the closet. She went one step further - she had the cabinet sealed shut. Essentially, she wanted to bury the memory of the horrific event yet preserve the final vestige of the slain leader.

That tragic night in Ford's Theater was only the beginning of Clara's nightmares.

Two years later, Clara married Henry Rathbone and eventually the couple had three children. When Grover

Cleveland became president he appointed Rathbone as his consul to Germany.

Over the years, Rathbone's behavior began to change and he literally became insanely jealous of Clara's attentions to the children.

Two days before Christmas in 1883, Rathbone murdered Clara in front of their children and then turned the gun on himself. He survived but was found guilty of murder. Rathbone was committed to an asylum for the criminally insane.

The Loudon house no longer exists, but for years Clara Harris' hysterical wraith haunted the dwelling. Not surprisingly, Abraham Lincoln's solemn specter appeared in the structure as well. Undoubtedly his life essence, brought back to Loudonville via Clara's bloodied dress, accounted for his post-mortem appearances.

## VAN HORN MANSION
### *Newfane*

In 1811 James Van Horn built the first gristmill along Eighteen Mile Creek in nearby Burt but a year later the British burned the mill during the War of 1812.

Undaunted Van Horn rebuilt the grist and saw mill five years later along with a log cabin for his family. Business flourished and in 1823, James erected a store, distillery, and an imposing brick house - today's Van Horn Mansion at 78th Street. He hosted the first town meeting there on April 6, 1824.

Another fire destroyed the grist but James restored the mill and went on to construct a woolen factory completed in 1842.

Eventually his two sons managed some of the properties. James Jr. took over the mill operation and Burt oversaw the house and farm. The hamlet of Burt is named after Burt Van Horn.

Burt Jr. remodeled the brick mansion in 1900 by building an addition and installing the leaded stained glass dome.

The house exchanged hands many times over the years and for a time served as a restaurant and an apartment house. Noury Chemical owned the property for ten years and during that time an employee spotted lights moving inside the house - investigators found no one inside. Noury donated the mansion to the Newfane Historical Society in 1987.

The old manse suffered when vandals smashed its doors and windows as it stood vacant – *or was it?*

James Jr.'s wife, Malinda, was only 21 years old when she met with a swift and tragic death when she was struck by a falling tree limb in 1837. Her mortal remains were interred in nearby Cemetery Orchard but her spirit stands steadfast in watching over the family home from beyond the grave.

For years, there have been many Malinda sightings. Her visage was spotted looking out windows when the house was empty. A roofer was so startled to see her face staring out the windowpane that he almost fell off his ladder. Visitors outside the dwelling attest to hearing someone tapping on the glass of the upstairs window.

When the house was being restored, wallpaper hangers said Malinda stood watching them.

Another clue to an ethereal presence inside the domicile is dogs' reaction to the unseen. Animals are known to be great barometers when it comes to the supernatural. In the Van Horn mansion dogs bark, growl, raise their hackles, and refuse to enter the library.

The ghostly Malinda likes to pose in the street or sidewalk in front of her house - just as she did when she was alive. To this day some will not even drive by the mansion for fear of catching a glimpse of her ghost - they go miles out of their way to avoid passing by the spirited dwelling.

Malinda's ghost is harmless but an otherworldly encounter is an unforgettable experience. Some have come face to face with Malinda's full-bodied apparition; they claim her spirit manifests as a mist then slowly shifts into the shape of a woman. She'll linger for several seconds and then suddenly vanish.

## SHAKER SETTLEMENT
### *New Lebanon*

In the 19th century, many religious movements migrated to the Empire State. The Shakers, a devout and disciplined sect, established a settlement in New Lebanon. They constructed twenty wooden buildings along a narrow dirt road that was at the time the main thoroughfare between Albany and Boston.

Their leader, Ann Lee, came to America in 1774 to escape persecution in England. Initially they assembled in Watervliet, New York.

The Shakers were literally a spin-off of the Quakers – shaking, trembling, and whirling were integral to their religious practices; they believed the frenzied behavior would absolve their sins and rid them of bad habits.

The Shakers were meticulous craftspeople who excelled at building furniture; their creations are now highly sought antiques.

They practiced celibacy, which is why their sect eventually died out. The last Shaker left the area in the 1940s and their old community became a summer camp.

The Sufi Order of North America acquired the property in 1975 and set up the Abode of Message Center in the eastern half of the compound; the Darrow School occupies the westernmost territory.

The peaceful spirits of those who once inhabited the site visit both residents; the ghost of a woman wearing an apron was seen at the school and the Sufis "sense" the Shakers' leftover energy generated during their tenancy.

*Mysterious Niagara Falls*
*Winter Scene*

## NIAGARA FALLS

The legend of the Maid of the Mist is rooted in the lore of the Seneca Indians who inhabited the Niagara region long before the European explorers arrived. The falls were considered sacred and the home of deities.

Indians were dying and the Ongiara tribe felt that they must appease the Thunder God Hinum who lived with his two sons in a cave behind the falls. At first the Indians offered fruit, flowers, and game but the perishing continued. The Indians knew they must sacrifice the tribe's most beautiful maiden, Lelawala.

On the appointed day, Lelawala appeared on the riverbank above the falls wearing flowers and a white doeskin robe. She stepped into a white birch bark canoe and plunged over the falls to her death. Her heartbroken father leaped into his canoe and followed her.

Hinum's two sons caught Lelawala in their arms and each desired her. She promised to accept the one who told her what evil was killing her people.

The younger brother told her of a giant water snake that lay at the bottom of the river. Once a year, the monster snake grew hungry, and at night entered the village, poisoned the water, and devoured the dead.

Lelawala's spirit told her people to destroy the serpent. Indian braves mortally wounded the snake. Returning to his lair on the river, the snake caught his head on one side of the river and his tail on the other, forming a semi-circle and the brink of Horseshoe Falls.

Lelawala's spirit returned to the cave of the God Hinum where she reigns as the Maid of the Mist.

## ACKLEY HOUSE
### *Nyack*

*1* Laveta Place is a bona fide haunted house. That is according to the New York State Supreme Court.

The Hudson River property was the subject of a landmark court case that determined if a house is known to be haunted, that information must be disclosed in any New York State real estate transaction as a pre-existing condition.

In 1990 prospective buyers made a down payment for the Ackley house. When a local architect casually mentioned that the house was haunted, the buyers wanted out of the deal.

They found out that in the past, the owner had willingly shared the story of the ghosts occupying her home for an article in *Reader's Digest* and the house was featured as a stop on the local ghost tour.

The prospect of sharing space with a rosy-cheeked ghost or the specter of a Revolutionary War soldier was too much to bear for the potential buyers. They wanted their deposit back.

Mrs. Ackley refused to cancel the sale or return the deposit. The case went to court, all the way to the State Supreme Court. The judge ruled in favor of the buyers because Ackley had actively promoted her house as haunted, but when it came to selling the place, she failed to disclose the information.

## FORT ONTARIO
### Oswego

The British have a long history at the site of the "Fort of Six Nations" so it comes as no surprise that their official ghost is the revenant of a British soldier dressed in the typical red coat uniform worn during the Revolution.

Dubbed George Fykes, undoubtedly inspired by the name on a tombstone of a fallen private in His Majesty's Service, his phantom appeared to every new regiment for over a century. When witnessed, an icy chill signified his specter who walked about appearing dazed and confused apparently not realizing he was dead.

Another celebrated spirit at the garrison manifested as a ghostly light during World War II. Promptly at midnight a ball of light, about the size of a saucer, would hover over the head of the guard on duty and keep pace with the sentry for the duration of his watch.

Was this the essence of a long ago soldier still on the lookout? Whatever it was left the post when the fort was decommissioned after the war. Well, not exactly...

In a few of the buildings, inveterate ghost hunters, equipped with electromagnetic field detectors and infra-red cameras, have registered high levels of electromagnetism and captured on film dozens of mysterious light orbs indicating the presence of an invisible energy source.

Fort Ontario State Historic Site dates from 1755. Today, visitors experience the star-shaped fort restored to its 1867-1872 appearance and perhaps sense the leftover spirits still stationed at the remote outpost.

*Raynham Hall*

## RAYNHAM HALL
*Oyster Bay*

Raynham Hall dates to 1740 when it was center of local affairs in Oyster Bay and home to the prominent Townsend family. In 1913, Julia Weeks Cole, the first to document the ghostly goings on, purchased the estate.

John André, a British major during the Revolutionary War is one of Long Island's best-known ghosts. He has haunted this 260-year-old saltbox house at 20 West Main Street for over 200 years.

General Benedict Arnold, in reward for his bravery at Saratoga, was placed in charge of West Point, an important fortification on the Hudson River positioned to protect northern New York from attack. But Arnold, believing that he had not received enough recognition for his services, plotted to turn the fort over to the British. Fortunately, for America, his scheme was thwarted.

During the British occupation of Oyster Bay in 1778, André spent many hours at Raynham Hall visiting with the Townsends who were sharing their home with British Commander Lieutenant Colonel John Simcoe.

One day as André conferred with Simcoe, Sally Townsend overheard them scheming about a payment to Benedict Arnold for the surrender of his troops. Through their connections, the Townsends managed to relay the treasonous plot to George Washington.

André was apprehended at the rendezvous spot, caught red-handed with Arnold's missive, and executed. André has haunted Raynham Hall ever since. (Arnold fled to England for refuge and died in London in 1801.)

Julia Cole wrote in 1938 that she awoke in the middle of the night, looked out the window and spied the ghost of a man on horseback; she suspected it was André.

It is claimed that at least once a year the ghost of a shaggy looking young man, wearing a dark woolen coat with brass buttons and smoking a pipe, walks in the garden. In the house, near the main staircase, a ghostly thin man with facial hair, wearing a dark jacket puts in an appearance from time to time. Staffers deduce that these manifestations are Michael Conlin, an Irish immigrant who worked at the home as a servant in the 1860s.

Another Raynham Hall spook is supposed to be Sally Townsend. They say that Sally was in love with John Simcoe, but the commander betrayed her affections. Sally died a spinster at the age of 82 and her unhappy spirit remains in the house. Her bedroom on the second floor is constantly icy cold, even during the summer.

The ghost of a servant woman materialized on at least one occasion in the kitchen. She could be the spirit responsible for the delicious scent of baking apples quite commonly experienced.

Electronic voice phenomenon (EVP) recorded at the site by Long Island ghost investigators documented spine-tingling voices saying, "Yes, there is," "Be patient," "Yes... I am," "I'm mad at you," "Shhhhhh," and "I want outta here" in response to the researchers' questions.

Other traces of paranormal phenomena include the smell of whiskey at times, and a rosy aroma wafting through the historic, and *very* haunted, home.

## STORM KING HIGHWAY
### *Rockland County*

One of the most colorful characters in American history is Revolutionary War General "Mad" Anthony Wayne. His ghost frequents a number of places in the northeast, but his most dramatic haunt is NY Route 218.

Also known as Storm King Highway, the scenic drive along the Hudson River offers what some consider the "Rhine River Vista of America," and a supernatural glimpse of history.

In 1779, George Washington counted on Wayne, and his trusted mount "Nab," to ride alone at midnight and warn the troops stationed at Storm King Pass of an impending attack. Wayne accepted the challenge and witnesses declared that blue and orange sparks flew out from the stallion's hooves as they struck the road.

Wayne outmaneuvered the enemy, and returned just in time to take command of a bayonet attack on Stony Point. This was the event that earned him the nickname "Mad" Anthony as well as the promotion to Major General.[7]

River dwellers allege that on certain gloomy nights, much like the night of Wayne's wild midnight ride, a dark cloaked figure on a phantom steed flashes along the narrow passage on Storm King Mountain, its presence signaling a stormy night.

---

[7] James Reynolds, *Ghosts in American Houses.*

## FORT STANWIX
### *Rome*

The site of Fort Stanwix in Rome was an Oneida "carrying place," an Iroquois Nation portage used to bridge the waterways. The stronghold was built in 1758 to safeguard the Mohawk Valley's major thoroughfare during the French and Indian War.

During the American Revolution, British military forces were driven back while attempting to capture the fort. American militiamen and Oneida allies attempted to come to the aid of Fort Stanwix but were ambushed at Oriskany, one of the bloodiest clashes of the war.

A colorful chapter in the history of our flag occurred when the defenders of Fort Stanwix decided to fashion one to fly over the fort. For the blue, they used a cloak captured from a British officer, regular army shirts served for the white stripes and stars, and material for the red, legend says, came from a woman's red flannel petticoat.

Much like the ghostly goings-on at several other ancient New York forts, spectral soldiers in period dress materialize in various places throughout the garrison. At sunrise, musical strains from phantom fifes and drums sometimes filter from the fortress and echo in the valley.

Other phantom fare at the fort includes the sound of a woman's wraith weeping. Tourists allege to have spotted the spirit of a one-legged man sitting in the barracks and an unseen spirit carries on his chores from the great beyond evidenced by the cleanly swept floors and supply of newly chopped wood.

## JACKSON GARDENS
*Schenectady*

The story of the Maiden of Jackson Gardens is a legend that has endured for over 300 years.

The story begins in 1672 with a young woman named Alice and her domineering father Jan Van der Veer, a merchant in the flourishing Dutch settlement. Although Alice was a charming and beautiful girl who had several potential suitors, Van der Veer forbade her to date.

One young man was determined, however, and he arranged secret trysts near Hans Groot's Kill, the brook that meanders through today's Union College campus.

One evening, the cruel Van der Veer, armed with a shotgun, followed the couple to their meeting place and shot the boy through the heart. He grabbed his hysterical daughter and dragged her home. Outraged townsfolk apprehended Van der Veer, tied him to a stake, and set him ablaze.

During the fracas, an inconsolable Alice returned to her lover's lifeless body. Thinking she partnered with her father in committing the murder, the angry mob bound her to a stake and burned her on the spot - the place in Jackson Gardens, where on the first full moon after the summer solstice, the spirit of the Maiden is said to roam.

Over the years, the sighting of Alice's apparition has declined, but those who experienced her earthbound spirit claimed they smelled the scent of smoke prior to her spectral appearance.

## SENECA FALLS HISTORICAL MUSEUM
### *Seneca Falls*

The first women's rights convention in the United States was held at Seneca Falls in 1848 led by two New York residents - Susan B. Anthony and Elizabeth Cady Stanton. They appealed for women's right to vote, to be educated, and to own property in their own names.

The Seneca Falls Historical Museum, at 55 Cayuga Street, is housed in a 23-room Queen Anne Style mansion and was founded in 1896. Women's history highlights its collection.

As you would expect, the museum provides an equal opportunity setting to its phantom population providing a haven to spirits of both sexes.

Edward Mynderse, son of the early land developer Colonel Wilhelmus Mynderse, resided in the family domicile living off his inheritance until his death.

When the Becker family moved in and remodeled the 1855 house, the renovation awakened Edward's sleeping spirit. Generally, much like people, ghosts don't take kindly to change, and it appeared that Edward was none too pleased. Doors opened and closed on their own, unexplainable noises were heard, furnishings and paintings were moved around, and clocks went cuckoo.

The museum staff welcomes Edward's spirit for they feel he watches over his mortal abode and the mortals who run it. Tour leaders always acknowledge his presence and share stories of his antics, which include tossing stuffed animals and removing tacks from the storm window plastic.

Psychics intuit that another spirit present in the house is a young Irish maid who died of tuberculosis when she was only 14. In their mind's eye they discerned the heartbroken girl crying on the back stairs because she longed to return to Ireland to be with her parents.[8] Ghosts hang around because they don't realize they're dead; the psychic informed the forlorn child that she needed to pass over to the Other Side.

The Becker family lived in the grand home for 70 years and employed a live-in maid named Mary who was quartered on the third floor. Her responsibilities included caring for the children. Mary delighted in fantasy and dressing the children in costumes.

After many years of faithful service Mary began to lose her faculties and the Beckers placed her in a rest home called the Willard State Hospital.

One evening, Mary showed up in the living room wearing her uniform. The Beckers sent her up to bed with the intention of returning her to the mental facility the next day. When they went to rouse her in the morning, she was gone and the room looked untouched. As they pondered this mystery the phone rang - it was the hospital calling to inform them that Mary had passed away the night before at 8:10 PM - the exact time Mary appeared in the living room.

Recently, workmen got goose bumps when a ghostly maid and costumed lass showed up to watch them work.

---

[8] David Pitkin, *Ghosts of the Northeast.*

*O* monstrous! O strange! We are haunted.

~ *A Midsummer's Night Dream*

*Split Rock Quarry*

## SPLIT ROCK QUARRY
### *Solvay*

On April 18, 1918, an industrial accident at Split Rock Quarry just west of Syracuse took the lives of fifty men and injured one hundred others.

In an effort to keep up with war-time demands, Solvay Processing Company was operating 24 hours a day mining and processing ore and extracting minerals vital in the production of picric acid, a bitter, toxic, yellow crystal used to make TNT.

During the nightshift, a gear overheated sparking a fire that rapidly spread and caused the explosion that took the lives of so many. Fifteen victims were never identified and they were buried in a common grave.

More than eighty years after the plant blew up, the spirits of the fifteen dead men were spotted roaming the ledges and standing on the ruined rock crusher of the old quarry. Their apparitions glowed yellow-green - a ghostly residue of the effects of the picric acid that once stained their skin chartreuse.

*Country House Restaurant*

## COUNTRY HOUSE RESTAURANT
### Stony Brook

Annette Williamson sided with the British during the Revolutionary War and her allegiance cost Williamson her life. She was hanged as a spy by loyalist troops and buried next to her kin in a small cemetery somewhere on the property now occupied by the Country House Restaurant on Long Island.

The woman's spirit usually makes her presence known in the kitchen area and her apparition has also been witnessed on the U-shaped staircase leading upstairs.

Once a towel floated by several witnesses and a news reporter had a glass of wine thrown in his face by the perturbed spirit.

The building on Route 25A was originally constructed in 1710 by Obadiah Davis as a farmhouse. Eventually the structure became an inn and stagecoach stop. In 1838, Thomas Hadaway, an English actor and comedian, bought the house and named it the Hadaway House Restaurant.

The present day rustic restaurant opened in 1967 and has been a reputed haunted spot for many years.

Parapsychologists have investigated the spooky allegations and purportedly contacted the spirit of a young woman who claimed that she and her family lived in the old house. She said she was the last of them to die - lynched for her disloyalty during the War for Independence.

## LANDMARK THEATRE
### *Syracuse*

Architect Thomas W. Lamb described his 1928 Loew's State Theatre as "European, Byzantine, and Romanesque." Opened near the close of the "roaring twenties," the theatre presented famous stage acts and first-run movies. When the stock market crashed, the show palace offered a temporary respite from the despair of the depression.

As theatergoers were ushered into the main lobby they delighted in the glow of a Louis Comfort Tiffany chandelier just like the one designed for Cornelius Vanderbilt's mansion, and were awed by the theater's grand murals. Musicians, seated in the gallery located over the front doors, serenaded the crowd during intermissions.

The showplace was decorated in rich reds and golds and embellished with lavish wall ornaments throughout. A 1,400-pipe Wurlitzer organ offered the exotic tones of glockenspiel, marimba, bird whistles, hoof beats and surf sounds.

Unfortunately, like so many other great movie palaces, attendance steadily declined. By 1975, it seemed inevitable that the pride of Syracuse would fall victim to the wrecker's ball.

Luckily, in 1977 a group of concerned citizens formed the Syracuse Area Landmark Theatre, or SALT. The grass roots organization recorded the illustrious theatre on the National Register of Historic Places. This prestigious designation opened the door to all kinds of much needed government funding.

When the group began restoring the showplace the volunteers and staff could never have imagined that they would breathe new life into long-gone theatergoers.

In the upper balcony, employees encountered a pale young female dressed entirely in white. When the ushers politely asked her to leave the area she faded from their sight. Psychics intuit that she is the spirit of a woman who worked at the theater and spent all her life longing to perform on stage.

Another spirit haunting the palace is an electrician who once worked at the theater. Oscar Rau's ghost has been observed near the light board.

Many have witnessed a mysterious blue light throughout the theatre but especially near the banister running along the back of the auditorium, in the catwalk access hallway, and on the stairs leading to the downstairs dressing room.

Some intuitives claim that the Red Room still tingles with the passionate energies of the players involved in a violent love triangle.

The basement is off limits to the timid as is the Walnut Room - both areas are plagued with inexplicable cold spots.

Today, the theater continues its restoration and fundraising efforts, while offering the Syracuse area a full schedule of performances by the living - and the dead.

Our revels now are ended. These are our actors,
As I foretold you, were all spirits, and
Are melted into air, into thin air.

~ William Shakespeare, *The Tempest*

*Sunnyside*

## SUNNYSIDE
### *Tarrytown*

Washington Irving's *Legend of Sleepy Hollow* is one of the nation's best-known ghost stories. Irving based his story about the ghoulish rider on an actual apparition he heard about while serving as a tutor in a mansion near Kinderhook.

Not surprisingly, Irving's spirit now inhabits "Sunnyside" his treasured pre-Civil War estate on White Plains Road.

In 1835 the author purchased the property with the small Dutch farmhouse and transformed the house into a cozy home he liked to call his "snuggery." Nestled in the historic Hudson Valley, Irving's "Sunnyside" is an original, much like the man himself. His vine-covered home contains the writer's books, furnishings, and memorabilia.

Gentlemen in top hats and ladies in hoop skirts welcome tourists to Sunnyside - a visit there is like a step back in time and into another world, literally.

Irving's ghost, as well as those of his nieces who used to take care of the place, reportedly haunt the national landmark. The three-story tower known as the "Pagoda" is the author's favored haunt. The phantom nieces are noted for their after hours tidying up.

Irving's nephew Pierre lived in the Tarrytown home after his uncle's death and reported that one evening, while he was sitting in the living room with his two daughters, Irving walked right pass them, as plain as day, and entered his study.

*T*he distance that the dead have gone
Does not at first appear -
Their coming back seems possible
For any an ardent year.

~ Emily Dickinson

*The Pink House*

## THE PINK HOUSE
### *Wellsville*

*E*dwin Bradford Hall descended from ancestors who arrived in America on the *Mayflower*. Hall, a lumber merchant by trade, arrived in Wellsville in 1852 and built a home inspired by the villas near Lake Como, Italy. He had the home painted pink and the color remains so to this day in accordance with tradition.

The haunting tale of the Pink House has several versions but they always begin with Hall's two daughters.

One story is that Pauline had a secret love who came from the wrong side of town. Only once did he go to the Pink House and when Mr. Hall saw him, he called the boy a "beggar." The boy left for school and the couple corresponded until the father intercepted the letters. Hall forged two bogus notes of his own and sent them to the lovers, which effectively ended the romance.

Pauline found another love and the day before their wedding, she passed her true love on the street and he ignored her. Broken-hearted, she returned home and drowned herself in the marble fountain in front of the house.

Although Pauline was absent physically her spirit remained behind. Some sensed her presence in the library and often found Elizabeth Barrett Browning's *Sonnets from the Portuguese* lying open on the table and the room scented with Pauline's favorite perfume. Strains of her favorite piano pieces sometimes filtered through the rooms.

Another account claims the young man betrayed Pauline by marrying her sister, triggering Pauline's suicide in the fountain.

The day came when the errant couple returned to the Pink House to live. The father had no choice but to forgive them for he had already lost one daughter.

The couple soon blessed the patriarch with a granddaughter who was the apple of his eye. As a toddler, however, she became morose and withdrew to the garden where her phantom aunt frequently appeared.

The story goes that one night Pauline's spirit coaxed the tot into the fountain. Her lifeless little body was found by the grief stricken grandfather the next morning.

Believing the house was cursed, the couple left only to return two years later, with another daughter, to take care of the aging Hall. This time, to ward off Pauline's ghost, they always left the lights on in the house at night.

Mason Winfield relates in *Shadows of the Western Door*, that on a September afternoon in 1907, Hall's daughter found her second child lying dead in the fountain. Her paralyzed, grief-stricken father was in his wheelchair on the front porch rocking in anguish, a helpless witness to the death of yet another innocent.

According to subsequent owners, since the Halls left the dwelling, and the fountain was removed, nothing out of the ordinary disturbed those living in the Pink House. Yet there are townsfolk who insist that there's an ethereal presence about the house that manifests as a light in an upper window...

## U. S. MILITARY ACADEMY
### *West Point*

West Point is the nation's oldest military post in continuous operation. General George Washington considered the imposing plateau on the west bank of the Hudson River the most crucial strategic position in America. He handpicked Thaddeus Kosciusko, a hero of Saratoga, to design the fortifications in 1778.

During the Revolution, West Point served as Washington's headquarters. In order to safeguard the important waterway, an 150-ton iron chain was extended across the sharply angled Hudson to Constitution Island, preventing passage by the British.

The British, despite Benedict Arnold's betrayal, never captured the fortress.

Since 1802 the nation's army officers have been trained at the austere academy. Graduates, headed by generals such as Grant, Lee, Sherman and Jackson, set high standards of military leadership during the Civil War for both the North and South.

Eisenhower, MacArthur, Bradley, and Patton, were among an impressive array of Academy graduates who met the challenges of leadership in World War II.

On the other hand, one-time cadets, Edgar Allan Poe and James Whistler, opted for alternative careers.

Colonel Sylvanus Thayer, considered the "father of the Military Academy," served as Superintendent from 1817-1833. In his superintendent quarters, it appears that his Irish cook "Molly" has never left.

The distinction between past, present, and future
is only an illusion, however persistent.

~ Albert Einstein

*West Point*

Legend says that when Molly died, a mysterious mark suddenly appeared on the kitchen breadboard; she obviously wanted to be remembered. The son of another superintendent awoke during the night and saw a woman in a long white dress standing over his bed. As he watched, she turned and disappeared through a closed door. Messing up newly made beds is another one of Molly's unearthly antics.

A black ghost in the General's Quarters is a soldier from the 1800s. His playful spirit pilfers valuables such as money and jewelry and deposits them in the master bedroom.

In the 1920s, servant girls living in West Point's Morrison House bolted from the residence screaming that a female ghost was chasing them. The woman who caused their terror was the dead wife of a professor who broke a promise to his dying wife and married her mother; the wife raged from beyond the grave.

The most documented case of paranormal activity happened in 1972, when several cadets witnessed the luminous apparition of a 1830s soldier. He was dressed in an old-fashioned uniform consistent with that of a 19th century Cavalry fighter and sported a handlebar mustache. The ghost materialized in Room 4714, looked at the fledgling soldiers, then turned on his heels and walked through the wall.

Those who experienced the eerie event said that a rapid drop in temperature that turned the room icy cold preceded the specter's appearance.

Administrative officials took into account the academy's long-established Cadet Honor Code, which prohibits lying, and took the sightings seriously. The room is off limits and used only for storage.

*T*he boundaries which divide Life from Death,
are at best shadowy and vague.
Who shall say where one ends,
And where the other begins?

~ Edgar Allan Poe

*French Castle, Fort Niagara*

## FORT NIAGARA
### *Youngstown*

On a high bluff overlooking the Niagara River sits one of the oldest forts in the United States - a garrison once occupied by four nations at different times - France, Great Britain, Canada and the United States. The nation who conquered this strategic location controlled access to the Great Lakes and the westward passage.

The oldest structure at the complex is the French Castle built upon Fort Conti, a stronghold established here in 1678 by French explorer LaSalle.

There are historians who claim that the fort is constructed on top of up to one hundred previous structures dating from 160 A.D. when an early Native American tribe constructed one of twelve known forts.[9]

The battle of Fort Niagara occurred in 1759. An oft-told folktale is that during the two-week siege a pair of Frenchmen quarreled over a woman. Their dispute was so severe that there was only one way to settle the contest - a swordfight would put an end to the enmity.

The dueling men relentlessly clashed with each other. Finally, with a ghoulish flourish the victor savagely decapitated his opponent. The story goes that Henri LeClerc's bloody skull rolled down the cobblestones and into a well.

Legend has it that on moonlit nights LeClerc's headless apparition rambles about the French Castle, or roams the battlements, looking for his severed head.

---

[9] Mason Winfield, *Shadows of the Western Door.*

(Talk about losing your head over a woman...) this story was in print by 1839 but it's doubtful that it's true.

The earliest report of the paranormal was in 1815 when a "hobgoblin," an elemental spirit, appeared in the cemetery. In the 1980s another entity revealed itself on videotape as a filmy image flitting behind the mortals.[10]

Fort Niagara is noted as the most haunted site in Western New York. The paranormal reputation is bolstered by the sounds of disembodied footsteps, creaking doors, and "creepy" feelings experienced by staff and visitors.

Overnighters felt transported to an earlier time through lucid dreaming and a reporter who braved the night here heard the definite sound of kitchenware, chairs scraping the floorboards, and soldiers marching, praying, and snoring.[11]

At Halloween, the historic site celebrates its otherworldly notoriety by offering ghost tours and scary campfire tales events.

---

[10] Ibid.
[11] Ibid.

## ACKNOWLEDGEMENTS

Deeper studies of the paranormal are on going and there are those who assert that encountering the unknown can lead to personal transformation. To this I can attest.

My lifelong dream was to make a living as a writer. My encounter with Grace Brown's ghost in upstate New York was the catalyst for chronicling true ghost stories. I owe her spirit a world of thanks.

Also, I want to express my appreciation to all those who have assisted in my research and to all my readers.

Particularly I want to thank my special friends for the role they played ...

Patricia Cañete                    Susan Grahn
Bridget McMahon Carles      Ann Marie Macken Peña
Julio Del Castillo, M. D.       Deborah Maldonado
Debbie Devrous                   Christine Schmelzle

# BIBLIOGRAPHY

Blackman, W. Haden. *The Field Guide to North American Hauntings*. Three Rivers Press, New York, NY; 1998.

Brown, Sylvia, *Visits from the Afterlife*. Dutton, New York, NY; 2003.

Cohen, David, *Encyclopedia of Ghosts*. Dorset Books, New York, NY; 1984.

Hauck, Dennis William, *National Directory of Haunted Places*. Penguin Books, New York, NY; 1996.

Holzer, Hans, *Ghosts, True Encounters with the World Beyond*. Black Dog & Levanthal Publishers, New York, NY; 1998.

Jones, Louis C., *Things That Go Bump In The Night*. Syracuse University Press, Syracuse, NY; 1983.

Kavanau, Ted, "Haunted Property." *lexisONE*; 2001. (www.lexisone.com)

Mead, Robin, *Haunted Hotels*. Rutledge Hill Press, Nashville, TN; 1995.

Merritt, Jim, "Stalking Specters." *NEWSDAY*, Long Island, NY; October 29, 2000.

Moran, Michael & Scott, Beth, *Historic Haunted America*. Tor Books, New York, NY; 1995.

Myers, Arthur, *A Ghosthunter's Guide*. Contemporary Books, Chicago, IL; 1993.

_____, *The Ghostly Gazetteer*, Contemporary Books, Chicago, IL; 1990.

_____, *The Ghostly Register*, Contemporary Books, Chicago, IL; 1986.

Pierce, Frederic, "New York's Haunted Havens." *The Post-Standard*, Syracuse, NY; October 26, 2003.

Pitkin, David J., *Ghosts of the Northeast*. Aurora Publications, Salem, NY; 2002.

Reynolds, James, *Ghosts in American Houses*. Paperback Library, New York, NY; 1967.

Winfield, Mason, *Spirits of the Great Hill*. Western New York
  Wares, Buffalo, NY; 2001.
_____, *Shadows of the Western Door*. Western New York Wares,
  Buffalo, NY; 1997.
Zezima, Jerry, "In Spirited Company." *NEWSDAY*, Long
  Island, NY; October 25, 1998.

## Websites:

Athenaeum Hotel: www.athenaeum-hotel.com
Bannerman Island History: www.hudsonriver.com
Belhurst Castle: www.belhurstcastle.com
ENJOY! The Hudson Valley: www.pojonews.com
Getting Curious about the Past: www.lihistory.com
Ghosts of Beardslee Castle: www.beardsleecastle.com
The Ghost of Nyack: www.members.home.net
Ghosts of Western New York: www.wnygoth.com
Haunted New York: www.hauntedny.com
Haunted Places in New York: www.shadowlands.net
Historic Cherry Hill: www.historiccherryhill.com
Hyde Hall: www.hydehall.org
Landmark Theatre: www.landmarktheatre.org
Legend of the Maid of the Mist: niagarareporter.com
Long Island Ghosts: www.hauntedlongisland.com
Newfane Historical Society: www.niagaracounty.org
New York Ghosts: www.hauntedlongisland.com
New York State Assembly: www.assembly.state.ny.us
Old Fort Niagara: www.oldfortniagara.org
Selkirk Lighthouse: www.maine.com
Seneca Falls Historical Society: www.sfhistoricalsociety.org
U.S. Military Academy at West Point: www.usma.edu
The White Inn: www.whiteinn.com

Other *ghostly*

Titles by *Lynda Lee Macken*

ADIRONDACK GHOSTS ~ Volumes I & II

GHOSTLY GOTHAM
New York City's *Haunted* History

HAUNTED HISTORY OF STATEN ISLAND

HAUNTED SALEM & BEYOND

GHOSTS OF THE GARDEN STATE
Volumes I & II

HAUNTED CAPE MAY

HAUNTED BALTIMORE

BLACK CAT PRESS
Post Office Box 1218, Forked River, New Jersey 08731

E-mail: llmacken@hotmail.com